THE FLIGHT OF A MARKETER

From Takeoff to Triumph

AMIT JAIN

ISBN
Paperback 979-8-89699-501-2
Hardcase 979-8-89777-610-8

Acknowledgements

To say this book is by me would be an overstatement. It is the outcome of the inspiration I received by working with so many wonderful professionals throughout my career so far. I dedicate this book to each one of them.

To my parents, who brought me up with deep values of appreciating small things in life and never stopped me from exploring myself. Their belief in me gave me the confidence to step out and find my way.

To my siblings, Anand and Monika, who were always smarter than me (even today), and I, being the middle child, had something to learn from both.

Special note to my teachers and professors who prepared me to face real-world encounters and infused courage in me to try things that I could never imagine myself doing.

Finally, and most importantly, to my lovely wife, Rashmi, who has been my strongest support in the past 19 years of our married life and to my adorable daughters, Khanak and Aarvi. They have been my deepest and most enduring support. They are my biggest supporters and my biggest critics as well. They complete me. I am deeply thankful to them.

Contents

Contents

<hr>

Introduction

About Me

Marketing: A Dream Job

2001, Nagpur, India. I still remember the day I started my MBA programme in this beautiful city of Maharashtra and the very first experience for me stepping out of my comfortable life with my parents. I had just finished my Bachelor of Commerce in my hometown, Kanpur, the so-called industrial town in the North of India.

After being brought up in Kanpur and spending 21 formative years of my life there, I was all by myself to start working on my dream – to become the top marketer in the country, which I articulated during my interviews as "to be the CMO of a multinational company in India". Yes, that was my dream job at 21 years of age!

My two years in the Department of Management Studies and Research at Tirpude College in Nagpur were nothing more than a dream come true. Expert professors, great colleagues, long night-outs and a long-distance relationship (☺ *maybe a separate book on this topic*).

When I came out of the college with 2 years full of excellent remarks from our professors (one being my favourite even after all these years - "*Amit can take marketing classes in my absence*" came from our dear marketing professor Mr. Lalit Khullar) and an MBA degree with flying colours, the reality was '*I had no job in hand!*'

Not that the college didn't have a placement cell; I was not taken by any company that came to our college that year. Maybe I was not job-ready. I was, but only in my thoughts.

My first job came to me courtesy of my one-week project during my second year of the MBA programme. I was one of the many who worked at a promotional stall for a consumer durable brand (Kentosh Electronics – A Videocon group company selling Toshiba brand of TVs and Kenwood music systems in India back then) during an electronics expo that earned me around 250 INR per day.

The branch manager in Nagpur liked my dedication and sent me for an open interview to their Mumbai office. Eventually, the company hired me as a management trainee in Mumbai, and there started my professional journey, which I can surely term as 'nothing less than a rollercoaster ride'.

Even now, over two decades later, when I look back at what I have been through, all my failures and all my achievements, I feel there has been a huge portion of luck that worked for me. No doubt I had put in all my efforts and was single-minded about my ambition (remember the CMO thing?), but being in the right place and at the right time makes a huge difference. Many times, that happened to me, and here I am where I am today- writing this book based on my real-world experiences over the last two decades. Again, this is something I never imagined myself doing.

About the Book

This book is not about me. Not about what I have achieved and what I couldn't. I am sure all of us have our own stories of resilience and how we have come so far and become who we are today! And every story is an inspiration.

This book is a story of the collective experience that I gained in the last two decades of working with thorough professionals and experts. Some have been industry stalwarts, and many have made me learn every single day of my professional life. People from different cultural backgrounds have distinctive dreams and ambitions for themselves.

This book is all about how I have seen marketing in my journey with all these people whom I worked and networked with. And 'how I think a marketer thinks.' Perspectives may differ, but I am excited to tell this 'Story of a Marketer' in anticipation of your interest and association.

So, let us fasten our seat belts. I would like you to take this flight with me and have as much fun as possible.

And after we land, write back to me if you can relate to this. This is a must for all those who do not understand what I have written. I need to know your side. Maybe the topic of the next book ☺.

Time to take-off!

CHAPTER 1

The Story that Every Marketer Will Tell You

How everyone around you is a better marketer than you

How many of you remember the first meeting in your office at your very first job? Especially the marketers!

You are fresh out of college, having studied how to make marketing strategies, build brands, and do big viral campaigns, and now you are in the real world full of people around you telling you what to do!

My first job was in Mumbai, where my professional life had just begun in 2003. The very first project that I got was to review print advertisements created by the advertising agency as per the brief shared by my manager. In reality, it was to coordinate with the agency, take printouts of various versions of advertisements, hand them to my manager for him to get feedback from the country manager and then take that feedback in writing to the ad agency by a local train. I made the same trip back to the office after getting corrections done and to see if those were good to go. Once this process was done (sometimes after multiple train trips in a single day), the final act involved delivering the high-resolution advertisement material on a CD to the printing publication's scheduling department and securing the desired page position. At that time, there was no super quick emailing of creatives and video calls like we have today. Everything had to be done in person! At least, for me!

While the project included a high level of coordination, the whole first-hand experience provided me with real-world insights into how advertisements were made and what went into the process. Something no one could have taught me in a classroom. However, as you would have noticed above, in the process, my manager, who was the marketing lead, never gave all feedback and approvals from his side. They were all given by the country manager, who was consistently telling him what to do. Traditionally, marketers were never the final decision-makers, and the fate of big ideas or innovative campaigns depended on a nod from senior management, where marketing was always a third or fourth priority. Most of the business decisions were made considering sales, operations, and business partner preferences.

Time has changed, and so have the organisations. Competence has taken a front seat over the sheer number of years in the organisation. Business operations have evolved and transformed into new and modern ways of working. We see more and more young and ambitious professionals climbing their way to leadership positions and taking decision-making roles that were out of sight until a few decades back. There are many examples around us with leaders younger than their team members, providing a fresh perspective to people who have a mental block due to their long and monotonous work experience. Even traditional family-driven businesses are hiring professionals to lead their companies into a new world of a much younger and globally exposed audience.

Overall, the marketing landscape has transformed as well. What worked in the early 2000s might be ineffective today. From traditional advertising to digital dominance, marketing has evolved to match consumer behaviour and technological advancements.

In the early 2000s, marketing heavily relied on TV commercials, print ads, and billboards. Businesses spent millions on newspaper ads and television spots to reach their audiences. However, with the rise of the internet, digital marketing took centre stage. Today, companies invest more in online platforms like Google Ads, social media, and influencer marketing than in traditional methods.

Social media was virtually non-existent in the early 2000s. MySpace was the first big social network, but it was Facebook, launched in 2004, that changed the game. Over time, platforms like Instagram, Twitter, LinkedIn, and TikTok became powerful marketing tools. Businesses now use social media for brand awareness, customer engagement, and targeted advertising.

Back in the day, marketing campaigns were broad and targeted large groups of people with the same message. Today, data analytics allows marketers to personalise content for specific audiences. Companies track user behaviour online and use AI-driven insights to deliver ads tailored to individual interests. This makes marketing more relevant and effective.

Traditional celebrity endorsements have been replaced by influencer marketing. People now trust online influencers, bloggers, and YouTubers more than traditional ads. Brands collaborate with influencers to promote their products in an authentic and relatable way. This trend has made marketing more personal and engaging.

In the early 2000s, having a website was enough. However, as search engines evolved, businesses had to focus on Search Engine Optimisation (SEO) to appear on Google's first page. Content marketing also grew, with brands creating blogs, videos, and infographics to attract and educate their audience. Today, high-quality content is key to building brand authority.

Online shopping has skyrocketed over the years. Platforms like Amazon, Shopify, and eBay have made e-commerce a major player in the marketing world. Mobile marketing has also grown, with businesses optimising websites for mobile users and using SMS and app notifications to reach customers instantly.

The Omnipresent Marketing Experts

The rise of digital tools, social media platforms, and access to vast amounts of data has created an environment where almost anyone can claim to be an expert in marketing. But the truth is, being a great marketer goes far beyond passing judgements on ads created by others or posting on Instagram. It's a mix of strategic thinking, creativity, empathy, and the ability to adapt quickly to ever-changing market trends.

At first glance, it's easy to see why many of us believe they are skilled marketers. Social media and content creation platforms make it simple for individuals to share their ideas, whether through blog posts, videos, or memes. With the right tools and a basic understanding of consumer behaviour, anyone can put together an Instagram story or write a catchy tweet that attracts attention. In fact, there's a sense of instant gratification associated with marketing in the digital age—likes, shares, and comments feel like a validation of one's marketing prowess.

The crux of the matter is that marketing is involved so much in our daily lives, and it is so subjective a topic that everyone thinks he/she is an expert. More importantly, the one who is professionally responsible for it should listen to everybody around.

We all are culprits of real-time judging the marketing messages that we see and term them as good or bad. And we do it with utmost authority. Most of the time, we pass super quick judgements for advertisements that we see in our everyday lives. A radically different type of print innovation (remember the radio device pasted on the full-page advertisement by an automobile brand in India!) or a TV commercial with a desi language to drive home a simple point-of-sale message (*Aap cheez dekhte hain, daam nahi /* You look at value, not the price). Without understanding the motive and the audience of the advertisement, we often react like – 'Who are those making these lousy ads' OR 'What a crap!'

All of us are consumers as well as marketers. All of us have an opinion on marketing.

Let us come to the other side of the story.

A Marketer's Reality

While everyone's opinion on marketing might be well-intentioned, it often overlooks the complexities of the field. Marketing is not just about creativity; it's also about data, strategy, and psychology. Professionals in this field spend years mastering concepts like market segmentation, consumer behaviour, and return on investment (ROI). The best marketing campaigns are a blend of art and science, balancing innovative ideas with hard metrics. Yet, these nuances are often invisible to the casual observer, who might reduce the success of a campaign to its catchphrase or aesthetics.

A marketer is in a continuous tussle with ideas and suggestions coming from all directions. Each day of the job. They are not mere ideas or polite suggestions; most of the time, they are pushed as if they were the best ones, and what you have been thinking and proposing is nothing more than theory.

All professional marketers have been in situations where they bring radical marketing strategies to make their brands stand out. But most of the time, what sees the light of the day is influenced by pure short-term justifications and how those new ideas are termed as nothing but theory and 'nice words' created by a bunch of marketers.

In my own experience and through my network of marketers across industries, I have come across several long-term brand-building measures being evaluated from a very short-term lens of immediate sales and ROI (Return On Investment). The longer-term ideas relate to the broader vision and are mostly hard to visualise in terms of outcome. What they need is conviction, which is a difficult thing to ask for when you are just focusing on today's results.

In typical sales-focused organisations, the marketing team suffers the most when it comes to qualitative and creative ideas. It becomes funny in many companies when the downturn in sales performance is purely linked to poor marketing, as the organisation is not able to attract new customers, and the brand relevance is lost over a period. Do these companies take a step back and reflect on –

Did we try to build a brand for tomorrow's customers?
Did we evolve to meet new customer preferences? What will keep us relevant in the long term?

And then there are companies (I have been fortunate to be a part of) that are more consumer-focused and tie every action to their overall vision (the 'why' part of it – Thanks, Simon Sinek, for spreading the word and bringing a lot of strategic focus on this).

Everything in such companies revolves around their purpose. The reason why they exist in the first place.

"When we know WHY we do what we do, everything falls into place.
When we don't, we have to push things into place."

– Simon Sinek

The places that do not push things into place and let things fall into their place are the dream ones for a true marketer who is more than excited to try new ideas, experiment with new social trends, and attract a completely different kind of customers that were a blind spot in the traditional approach.

The ubiquity of marketing also means that its failures are public. A poorly received campaign becomes a trending topic, with people dissecting what went wrong and offering their solutions. "Why didn't they just…" is a common refrain, as if hindsight alone is enough to qualify someone as a marketing guru. What these critiques often miss is the context—the behind-the-scenes constraints, the conflicting stakeholder opinions, and the rapidly shifting consumer trends that professionals must navigate.

At the same time, marketers themselves can learn from public opinions. After all, the audience's perspective is invaluable. A campaign that fails to resonate with its target audience is a failure, no matter how strategically sound it seems on paper. Listening to opinions—even those delivered without expertise—can offer unexpected insights or spark new ideas.

Ultimately, the fact that everyone has an opinion on marketing is both a challenge and a testament to the field's relevance. It's a reminder that marketing doesn't exist in a vacuum; it's shaped by the culture, experiences, and perceptions of the people it aims to reach. Navigating this sea of opinions is part of the marketer's job—balancing professional expertise with the wisdom, and sometimes the noise, of the crowd.

CHAPTER 2

The Lesser-Known Story

The never-ending debate between short-term and long-term

To be able to drive business by clearly distinguishing between the overall strategy and operational effectiveness is a critical skill. A strategy is what will steer you towards your bigger ambitions. Operational effectiveness is how you implement that strategy and stay on that path.

Many times, this simple point gets missed when you focus on short-term benefits.

Let's take an example.

During the busiest holiday seasons, an airline notices a drop in sales and a decline in consumer choice when it comes to scheduling family vacations abroad.

Their research with lost customers showed that their overall experience was not great, and the whole family experience was not joyful. They prepared a strategy to tackle the situation and to win back the customers.

Idea: *Make them feel special.*

'Delight families by upgrading their experience in economy class to the next level without additional cost.'

The Proposition

A standard offer for all customers flying internationally with their families.

'All kids flying in economy class get their meals upgraded to business class (depending on the sector they are flying).'

Intention

The airline knew that customers would love their families, especially kids, to get an elevated experience while still travelling economy. This would improve the airline's customer delight scores and bring back lost customers.

The Execution

The airline announced its *'Upgrade Programme for Kids'* four months before the peak festive season so that it could capture the booking window (usually three to four months before the trip) and make an impact. The programme received an overwhelming response from the customers as they were not supposed to pay for this elevated experience, and the proposition had a higher value than the competition airlines. The other airlines were caught by surprise, and they had no time for a counteroffer.

The whole experience was announced as a standard offer, not with a lot of disclaimers but, more importantly, not for a short period of time. Hence, the customers saw it as a promising proposition and not a marketing gimmick. As a result, the airline started observing an increase in sales from year-over-year comparisons, and the customer delight score started improving.

While the whole proposition was supposed to work as a game-changer to improve customer experience and enhance overall business operations for the airline in the long run, something didn't let that happen.

As the sales results started showing an early upward trend, increased costs in economy-class services began to worry the finance team. Instead of looking at the longer-term revenues that were expected to increase, they focused on a short-term increase in costs.

By the time the airline reached its next festive peak, the operations team, under cost pressure, started cutting corners by limiting in-flight meal upgrades to one child per family and by trying to discourage bookings by large families to keep costs down! Instead of capitalising on the unique customer offer and making it big over a period of time, the airline started receiving worse ratings in customer experience.

Eventually, the airline lost its strategic advantage in the market and couldn't hold the increase in revenue. Competitors started providing a better and sustained level of experience, which took away the uniqueness and differentiated customer benefits.

What do you think happened here?

A clear case of operational challenge diluting the strategy and thereby deviating from the road to achieving the overall objectives. The short-term view of operational benefits blocks the path to achieving long-term ambitions.

Short-term vs Long-term

The appeal of short-term strategies lies in their immediacy. For businesses facing tight cash flows, market entry challenges, or quarterly performance pressures, these tactics can be a lifeline. They offer measurable outcomes and the ability to pivot quickly based on performance. For instance, a startup launching a new product may rely on a targeted digital campaign to generate buzz and sales quickly. However, the downside is that short-term tactics often prioritise immediate returns over sustainable growth. When overused, they can lead to consumer fatigue, diminishing returns, and a lack of brand differentiation.

On the other hand, long-term brand building focuses on creating lasting value and emotional connections with consumers. It's about establishing a brand's identity, values, and trustworthiness in the minds of its audience. This approach includes investments in storytelling, consistent messaging, quality customer experiences, and brand equity. Successful examples include Coca-Cola's association with happiness and Apple's reputation for innovation and design excellence. These perceptions didn't materialise overnight; they were built through years of consistent effort and strategic decisions.

The strength of long-term brand building lies in its ability to create resilience. Brands with strong equity are better positioned to weather economic downturns, market disruptions, or competitive threats. They enjoy greater customer loyalty, pricing power, and advocacy. However, the challenge is that the results of long-term efforts are often intangible and harder to measure. Return on investment

(ROI) may take years to materialise, which can make this approach less appealing in environments that prioritise immediate results.

The key to success lies in striking the right balance. Short-term campaigns and long-term brand building should not be seen as mutually exclusive but as complementary strategies. For example, a brand can run a holiday promotion to boost seasonal sales while ensuring the campaign aligns with its overarching brand narrative. Similarly, digital analytics can be used to measure the performance of both short-term initiatives and the incremental growth of brand equity over time.

Consider this when you, as a marketer, devise a plan that aims to achieve the company's long-term objectives and is built to make the brand's presence stronger over a period. And when you want all forces to work to get the plan implemented, you start getting different other views and directions that are merely based on immediate benefits. They may not align well with the longer-term growth strategy on which your plan is based. Due to this, the overall business strategy gets compromised for the sake of gains that are only visible on an immediate basis. How would you handle that?

Now, let us see how a professional marketer deals with such everyday scenarios.

When a marketer starts getting such vague ideas and suggestions without people understanding the overall marketing strategy, the first thing that comes to their mind is: *'What the hell do you know about marketing, or Do you even understand what I am trying to do?'*

Believe me, every marketer hates to be schooled on how to do marketing. And yet, the school is ON every single day in his job unless he becomes the ultimate decision-maker. Maybe it doesn't even stop there. But that is the mindset I have no experience with. Wait until I become a CEO, and I will surely write 'How a CEO thinks'.

Coming back to our topic, no marketer loves to take marketing ideas from people with no marketing understanding. However, in a professional setting, one must work with people. Like it or not, ideas will keep coming in.

Let us name our marketer in this book, '**Punk**', and we will see how Punk goes through different stages of this flight from taxi to take-off to landing. And we visualise ourselves in Punk's shoes all this while. Are you with me?

Punk's Flight: From Take-off to Triumph

Punk graduated from a not-so-top-notch business school but did extremely well to get a top rank in the institution. He is passionate about marketing and started his professional life at a financial institution as a management trainee.

The Early Days

Punk's early days in the corporate world were a mix of excitement, confusion and reality checks.

Fresh out of business school, Punk arrived with big dreams—envisioning high-stakes strategy meetings, million-pound campaigns, and innovative marketing projects. The reality? He spent the first few weeks reading company policies, attending compliance training, and figuring out how to work the coffee machine without causing an office-wide blackout.

His workstation was strategically placed in a corner where he couldn't bother the real decision-makers. His laptop took 15 minutes to boot up, and his inbox was empty—except for company newsletters and IT security reminders.

Within the first month, he realised financial marketing is filled with jargon: "**assets under management**," "**liquidity ratios**" and "**derivatives**". In meetings, he nodded like he understood, then secretly Googled half the terms later. His first attempt at writing a product pitch sounded like a mix between a Shakespearean tragedy and an insurance manual.

Instead of designing flashy campaigns, he spent hours updating spreadsheets, tracking customer engagement data, and making PowerPoint slides that no one ever read. Occasionally, he got a thrilling assignment—like proofreading a 40-page report on mortgage-backed securities.

Months later, after countless rejections and revisions, one of his ideas—perhaps a catchy tagline for a loan campaign or an engagement strategy for digital banking—was implemented. The campaign wasn't groundbreaking, but seeing it go live made him feel like Don Draper.

By the end of the first year, he had learned three crucial things:

- Marketing in finance was more about **trust** than creativity.

- **Numbers matter** as much as (if not more than) ideas.

- **Building relationships** with colleagues was just as important as impressing the boss.

With a bit more confidence, a lot of caffeine, and a growing understanding of financial products, he was no longer just a trainee—he was now a marketer in the making.

Stepping Up to Bigger Roles

After spending a couple of years in his first job and having gained loads of confidence, he joined a large multinational FMCG (fast-moving consumer goods) organisation as an assistant brand manager.

He spent three years in the company working with the brand manager and worked on multiple product campaigns, gaining the reputation of a sharp, reliable, and extremely professional team member in the overall sales and marketing department.

As Punk was establishing himself in the organisation, his brand manager made a move to one of their competitor companies, and the position was offered to Punk. Call it luck or God's grace, but it was a gem of an opportunity that Punk grabbed with open arms.

His first assignment was a new product launch in a highly competitive skincare category. Punk prepared a comprehensive and well-thought-through marketing plan to launch his new product. He took all aspects of the business into consideration and consulted all the major stakeholders, including his marketing director.

However, as is the case with most marketers, he also couldn't escape from the ever-flowing waves of ideas and suggestions coming from people across different departments in the company. Some of the typical comments were:

The campaign message is not impactful. Nothing will happen. We need a better punchline.

This is not the right investment in this market. We should focus heavily on that region. That distributor supports us more.

Why are we not using this particular TV channel? The show on this one has many soap operas to attract female attention.

You do not know how things happen here. You are new and do not understand. Learn from us.

And the list went on…

Do you relate to any of the above comments? I am sure many of us do.

Let us see how our dear Punk handled this everyday situation and try to see if we can pick something from here.

So, the first strategy that Punk takes to deal with this is –

Swallow the Pill. Do Not Say NO to Anything

Simply put, it means being open and receptive to everything that is thrown at you but being very selective in what to pick up. A good marketer would not get into any argumentation and cross-reflection of pros and cons at that moment. Just let people share whatever they have to. This is exactly what Punk did. In most cases, people have random thoughts in their heads, and they just want you to follow them. And remember, things may not come at the same time or in one meeting. It is an everyday situation. He keeps them coming in an open jar that he has all the time.

The next step he took after receiving all the great ideas was to acknowledge and be thankful to the people around him. It is not an easy thing to do, but to sail through the corporate dynamics, it is important to hold your nerves and focus on your thing. A great marketer is one who handles it in a professional manner. It's not easy, but it's super important.

The major action Punk takes next is to analyse all the suggestions and come back with a clear response for each one of them. Sometimes, it is not possible for all, but he does it for most of them and for ease of handling – groups them with the nature of ideas.

1. Action for one group where the ideas would have 100% derailed the company from its path and made no sense to the current strategy – 'Clear NO'.

   He told them – "*Great ideas, but this doesn't fit well into our current strategy. Let's keep them with us and consider them later.*"

2. For another group which had some relevance, but Punk didn't see them getting incorporated into his plan – 'A Polite No.'

   He told them – "*Let's tweak these ideas and see how they fit into our current marketing strategy.*"

3.   For groups where ideas were too far-fetched, but these people have great influence in the company to be told a clear No. So, the action here was – Your ideas are too big, and we are not capable of executing them.

A careful message to them – "*We currently do not have the right resources and bandwidth for your ideas, but we will continue to follow up.*"

4.   And maybe for some ideas that really work – 'We take them'.

Punk accepted them wholeheartedly – "*Let us integrate this into our current marketing strategy and test it.*" (something might work as well)

So, what did he just do?

Instead of putting down the suggestions from others and making it a big corporate fight, all he does is give everyone a chance to pour their buckets on him, and he gets to decide what to pick. Well, he may still not be the final decision-maker because everyone has bosses, and they ultimately do what the boss says. But in this battle of wisdom coming from all directions, at least our poor marketer can manage the show and still go to the management with sheer conviction that '*With all his expertise and after listening to the stakeholders – Here is the marketing strategy that should work for the company.*'

With the above approach, did you notice what Punk was able to achieve?

His strategy is not killed. His plan stayed, and he still got to execute what he wanted.

And as a bonus, he is seen as an adaptable and open-minded professional. It is important for him to build his credibility to get more and more buy-ins for his future projects.

An achievement, I would say. What do you think?

Winning the (Inside) Arena!

Turning internal doubts into collaboration

Resistance is as much a part of corporate life as coffee breaks and Zoom calls. Whether you're introducing a new idea, changing processes, or just trying to get people to embrace a fresh perspective, resistance is bound to show up. It's like that one coworker who always has a "better way" of doing things—except this time, it's an entire workforce pushing back against change. But resistance doesn't have to be a brick wall. With the right approach, you can navigate it, address concerns, and turn sceptics into supporters. Let us see how Punk dealt with resistance and turned internal doubts into collaboration.

Punk stood in the bustling conference room, a stack of meticulously prepared presentations in one hand and a steaming cup of coffee in the other. It was launch week for his skincare brand, and the atmosphere was electric. Months of research, planning, and creativity had brought him to this moment. But Punk knew one universal truth about marketing: no plan, no matter how flawless, goes unchallenged.

We have seen how Punk navigated through the rough terrain of great ideas and suggestions to taxi his plane as he gets ready to take-off.

However, before he takes off on his strategy flight, he must ensure that he has all the ground staff and the ATC on his side. That is going to play a big part in making his journey successful.

While Punk has successfully dealt with the 'creative' lot and all the so-called thought leaders around him, there are the next set of 'question marks' who are always seen roaming around in the company and questioning everything that everyone is doing.

These are the great gatekeepers of the company's policies & guidelines and question everything that is different and beyond their limited periphery of imagination. It would be interesting to list some of the typical comments.

People Who Have a Pessimistic Approach

"This has never happened in the company, and we do not know the consequences if things go wrong."

Group of people who want to keep doing what they are doing

"We already have a tried and tested way for years. Why experiment for this major launch?"

People in a comfort zone with existing partners

"We already have our old suppliers and agencies. Why do we want this new bunch of start-ups?"

People who want to stick to traditional ways and have a closed mindset towards new ways of doing business

"What is the problem with our existing sales channel? Why do we need to sell online?"

How many of you can recognise such instances around you?

Take a moment to think about this lot in your current space, and then read on.

A marketer will always challenge the status quo and try to do something that hasn't been done before. Our dear Punk is also made from the same elements, and he keeps challenging the norm. He has been following the journey of great leaders and achievers, which has given him a solid foundation and a clear thinking process. His ambitious approach evidently comes out when he starts all his strategy proposals with a simple yet powerful statement:

'To achieve something that has not been achieved before, one must do things that have not been done before.'

Now, that is the biggest problem with this bunch of 'question marks'.

How would you handle such a situation of inside challengers?

Let's see what Punk does.

The approach that Punk takes is very familiar to all of us. And that is called '***diplomacy***'.

The first step is to understand what motivates them. People who are overtly stuck on processes and question everything are often motivated by the desire to reduce risk. They see business risk in almost every new thing.

So, Punk makes a smart move. Instead of pushing too hard, he **identifies the low-hanging fruit** that can be used to gain confidence and build trust with this set of people. He intentionally pauses a couple of existing and ongoing projects to get more efficiencies in place and calls for a pitch from suppliers. He knows that a slight delay in these projects won't matter much in the overall scheme of things. By doing this and restarting a few smaller projects with higher efficiencies, he wins trust that is going to help him immensely in this bigger strategy execution.

The next step is to bring **flexibility as a strategic advantage**. Instead of positioning flexibility as "breaking the rules", Punk presents it as a strategic choice that can improve outcomes.

Ultimately, what will win the senior management is higher outcomes with better efficiencies. And that is what Punk sells.

Instead of saying, 'We should try this new approach to achieve better outcomes', he advocates, '*What if we explored how we could adjust the process slightly to reduce bottlenecks while still meeting our end goals? Sometimes small changes can make a big difference in efficiency.*'

Once 'higher efficiency with higher outcomes' is on the table, the next move brings Punk out of this process net and gives him the licence to take-off.

He makes them **party to the strategy and involves them as stakeholders**. Believe me, this is something every single soul would like and be happy about. Once they get a stake in something new and substantial, they stop questioning its very basic fundamentals. Suddenly, they start seeing all the benefits to which they were turning a blind eye. Nothing wrong when the overall project is helping the organisation with its desired objectives.

Here is one conversation that Punk smartly handled. While he was making the final presentation to the management team, the head of product development asked:

"Punk, are we sure focusing on eco-conscious packaging as our main hook is the right move? It feels like every brand is doing that."

Punk smiled, unfazed. *"You're right that eco-consciousness is trending. But our edge is that we're not just sustainable; we're pioneering refillable skincare solutions in the premium segment. No one else is doing it at this scale. Customers who care about luxury and sustainability will notice. Why don't you join us in making this a true differentiator? It would be great to use your expertise."*

All Punk did was – instead of taking it head-on and pushing to get things implemented, he acknowledged the topics and involved the 'question marks' as part of the new strategy, and they started working as catalysts for change.

Handling resistance in the corporate world is all about balance. You need to stand firm where necessary but also remain adaptable and understanding. Here is a 10-point game plan to handle resistance:

1. Understand Why People Resist

People resist change for many reasons: fear of the unknown, comfort in old habits, lack of trust, or just because they weren't consulted in the decision-making process. Before you start trying to bulldoze your way through the resistance, take a step back and ask: *Why are they pushing back?* Understanding the root cause makes handling it much easier.

2. Communicate Clearly and Early

Ever had a company announce a huge change out of the blue and expected everyone to be thrilled? Yeah, that never works. One of the biggest reasons for resistance is poor communication. People need to understand what's happening, why it's happening, and how it affects them. So, communicate early, often, and in a way that makes sense to everyone—not just leadership.

3. Acknowledge Concerns Without Dismissing Them

When someone voices resistance, the worst thing you can do is brush it off. If employees say, "This new system will slow us down," don't just reply with, "No, it won't." Instead, dig deeper. Ask, "What specifically makes you feel that way?" This not only helps address genuine concerns but also makes people feel heard.

4. Involve People in the Process

People are less likely to resist change if they feel like they have a say in it. If you're rolling out a new policy, involve employees in the discussion. Gather feedback, ask for suggestions, and let them feel like part of the decision-making process. When people have ownership, they become advocates instead of roadblocks.

5. Find Champions for Your Cause

Every workplace has influencers—people others look up to and respect. Identify these champions and get them on board early. If key employees support the change, their endorsement will help convince the more sceptical ones.

6. Offer Training and Support

Resistance often comes from fear of incompetence. If people feel unprepared for a change, they'll resist it. If you're implementing a new software system, provide proper training. If it's a new policy, give clear guidelines and support. Make sure no one feels like they're being thrown into the deep end without a life vest.

7. Celebrate Small Wins

People like to see results. If you're making a big change, celebrate the small victories along the way. Acknowledge and reward progress. Did the new system save time this month? Give a shout-out in a team meeting. Did the new process improve customer satisfaction? Share the good news! When people see benefits, they become less resistant.

8. Be Patient and Persistent

Some resistance melts away quickly, while other pushbacks take time. You might need to repeat your message multiple times before it clicks. Keep the conversation open, keep listening, and don't get discouraged. Change is a marathon, not a sprint.

9. Lead by Example

If leadership isn't embracing the change, why should employees? If you're pushing for a new approach, make sure you're walking the talk. If it's a new policy, follow it religiously. If it's a new technology, use it yourself. People are more likely to follow suit when they see leadership genuinely committed.

10. Know When to Pivot

Sometimes, resistance isn't just about stubbornness – it's a signal that something needs adjusting. If the pushback is overwhelming, re-evaluate. Maybe the timing is wrong, or perhaps the approach needs tweaking. Being flexible doesn't mean giving up; it means being smart about execution.

At the end of the day, **People do not resist change. They resist loss.** The sense of losing something, their control, their authority, their importance makes them question everything and resist any new approach.

Once you make them a stakeholder in change and turn the loss factor into a gain proposition, you are ready to take-off. And that is what Punk did!

CHAPTER 4

The Take-off!

Getting the strategy in place and setting the ball rolling

"Build something 100 people love, not something 1 million people kind of like."

– Brian Chesky, co-founder and CEO, Airbnb

Implementing a strategy is as critical as planning it. I had read an article on strategy implementation that captured a perfect analogy, and it stayed with me. Here it goes.

'It is like the preparation of a great meal, which requires more than just a fabulous recipe (i.e., a strategic plan). It takes high-quality ingredients, the right equipment, and a capable team of chefs and servers working well together; all critical elements involved in the preparation and service (i.e., execution) of the meal.' So true!

And our dear Punk was now ready for his tryst with the board of management after putting together all the planning and getting rid of the internal challenges.

Punk has considered all the key ingredients that make a marketing strategy comprehensive and compelling:

- **Brand Strength, Product advantages and competitive edge, Market dynamics**

The proposition that makes his brand strong and gives an upper hand in the marketplace. So, he knows his brand well, which would be handy to craft his customer messaging.

- **Product Advantages and Competitive Edge**

How the new product is different and relevant to its consumers? What would make it a preferred choice over the stuff that is already out there and available? So, Punk has taken care of the product differentiation and distinctiveness.

- **Market dynamics and key regions to compete**

Which markets would allow the brand to strengthen itself and the product to click? Considering the skincare product he is launching, he has chosen the most upmarket regions where the take rate is expected to be higher and immediate.

- **Price-value equation and premium margin**

What kind of pricing will make the consumers choose the product, and can they charge any premium over its rivals? It is essential to price the product correctly. Something that Punk has picked up from his earlier stint with the financial institution.

- **Key messaging and overall communication plan.**

What would be the prime message to its customers, and which mediums will they have in their overall campaign? A well-crafted message as per its brand strength and product advantages in the market, together with a sharp media strategy to be where the customer is. In this campaign's case, more of an online presence as the main commercial channel is online.

● Investment matrix

What levels of investment would be needed at various phases of the campaign, and does he have the management buy-in to get the resources as per the phasing he desires? And, of course, some level of agility must be built into the investment plan to manoeuvre based on the performance.

While all the above detailed planning was going to make Punk's campaign super strong, the one thing that is close to his heart and vital for him to be successful was the **understanding of his audience and putting it right**. For Punk, hitting his brand message and product communication bang on his audience was of utmost priority.

For that matter, any great campaign, may it be in any industry, has become great by all of the above planning, but the two most important aspects that make good campaigns great are:

1. **Audience.** Are you talking to the right person?

2. **Messaging.** Are you saying what will make him tick?

Recall any marketing campaign that you consider to be great; it will have the above two things straight on, and the rest of the things work in tandem.

Two examples from my side which are considered to be among the greatest campaigns of all time:

Example 1: Nike – 'Just do it' (https://www.youtube.com/watch?v=p_xozТo6wrU&t=32s)

What made it successful: Nike identified an emotional connection with its audience and connected meaningful stories to its core values, such as motivation, inspiration, and healthy living. Nike's decision to integrate the company's value proposition with an emotionally-driven message made for a wildly successful marketing campaign.

Example 2: Snickers – 'You are not you when you are hungry' (https://www.youtube.com/watch?v=dbpFpjLVabA&t=26s)

<u>What made it successful:</u> This one is effective because it used comedy to highlight how their product, a quick and easy candy bar, was the perfect solution to a widely held problem of being "hangry". The brand identified a customer pain point and positioned Snickers as the sensible resolution.

Of course, if the product is not great and doesn't fulfil the promise made by the brand, it will eventually fail. However, without the above two things (the right audience and the right messaging), your customers would not even try your product. This is where the success story starts. How much longer and wider it can become depends on the product and promises that the team can keep.

Coming back to Punk's story. He had it all planned. Even the way he was going to measure the campaign's success. He knew that the success of this campaign was going to play a big part in his own success story within the company. So, he took care of everything –

- Using an analytics tool to track performance on a real-time basis

- Doing A/B testing to see which message resonates well with the audience and what is giving it more bang for the buck

- Adjusting campaign settings based on real-time feedback and opportunities

Something important that Punk learned the hard way during his financial stint was **to plan for the worst.**

Contingency Plan

Considering the high stakes in this campaign, Punk had prepared a contingency plan, an alternative approach which was somewhat different from his current ambitious and modern style of marketing the product, focusing on online sales.

With risks identified in the current plan, Punk designed a robust crisis management framework. At its core was a clearly defined escalation protocol: minor issues were to be handled by the team, while major crises were escalated to leadership. Punk ensured each team member understood their role, whether it was managing media relations, communicating with suppliers, or addressing customer concerns.

To further strengthen this framework, he developed a decision matrix to guide actions during emergencies. For example, if a supplier fails to deliver a key ingredient, the matrix outlined steps to source alternatives or adjust production schedules.

The alternative plan was supposed to come into the picture in case there was turbulence in the existing flight so that he could continue the journey and land safely at the desired location. The route was different (a blend of traditional and modern styles of media approach) but the contingency plan had Punk covered.

CHAPTER 5

The Green Signal

Persuading the Top Management

It was a big day for Punk!

He was in the boardroom to present his marketing strategy for one final approval. Months of meticulous research, hours of late-night brainstorming sessions, and countless revisions had culminated in this moment. His radical marketing strategy for launching the new skincare brand wasn't just ambitious—it was groundbreaking. But convincing the top brass of the company? That was an entirely different challenge.

The boardroom buzzed faintly with anticipation as the executives filed in. The usual pre-meeting small talk felt more restrained today. Punk, standing by the presentation screen, radiated a quiet confidence. His radical marketing strategy – a daring departure from the company's historically conservative playbook – was about to be unveiled. He knew this wasn't just a pitch; it was a gamble, one that could redefine the company's trajectory or shake his career.

Setting the Stage

Punk's last few successes had pushed the boundaries, but today's proposal was different – it wasn't about incremental improvements. This was a bold leap, a manifesto to revolutionise the brand's identity in a fiercely competitive market.

As the last executive took their seat, the CEO nodded at Punk. "All right, Punk. You've got the floor."

He took a moment to look at his audience, ensuring he locked eyes with key decision-makers. He began with a striking question: "When was the last time we didn't just meet market expectations but shattered them?"

A murmur rippled through the room. Punk didn't wait for a response. He clicked on the first slide, which displayed a timeline of the company's marketing campaigns over the past decade. "Here's our history. Solid campaigns. Steady growth. But no defining moment."

Establishing the Challenge

The next slide revealed industry trends and market disruptors. Punk highlighted how newer, nimble competitors were winning with bold narratives, authentic branding, and emotionally resonant campaigns. He paused at an image of a competitor's viral ad, showing real people sharing their skin struggles. The tagline read: *"Your Skin, Your Story."*

"This is where we're losing," he said, his voice firm. "While we focus on perfection, the world is moving towards authenticity. If we don't adapt, we'll fade into irrelevance."

The CFO, known for her measured approach, leaned forward. "Interesting, but authenticity is subjective. How do you propose we control the narrative while remaining credible?"

Punk welcomed the question. "By empowering our customers to tell their stories and integrating them into our brand. We include real people using real products in our campaign, without any overproduction or gimmicks. And here's the best part—authenticity doesn't require massive budgets, just a genuine connection."

Unveiling the Strategy

He clicked to the next slide. The headline read: *"The Skin Revolution."* Punk outlined a three-tiered strategy:

1. **Grassroots Marketing:** Focused on smaller, authentic influencer partnerships and user-generated content campaigns.

2. **Experiential Events:** Pop-ups and skincare workshops in target cities, emphasising personal connections.

3. **Digital Storytelling:** Leveraging short-form videos showcasing real customer journeys.

"Each element is designed to amplify trust," he explained. "No glossy perfection, just real results."

Addressing Concerns

The COO raised a hand. "These ideas are ambitious, but we've seen bold strategies fail. How do we mitigate the risk?"

Punk responded with a calm smile. "I anticipated this concern," he unveiled a detailed risk analysis, showing how incremental testing and pilot programmes could provide proof of concept before full-scale implementation. A pilot campaign plan appeared on the screen, complete with timelines, budgets, and ROI projections.

"This allows us to experiment in controlled settings while minimising exposure," he said. "And if the pilot doesn't work? We pivot."

The CEO, who had been listening intently, raised an eyebrow. "You're asking us to take a cultural leap, one that shifts how we've marketed for decades. Why should we believe this will resonate with our audience?"

Punk leaned forward, his voice calm but impassioned. "Because the data supports it, and our competitors are proving it works." He clicked on a slide filled with consumer insights: survey responses, social media trends, and focus group feedback.

"We surveyed over 1,000 potential and existing customers," he explained. "Eighty-three percent said they're more likely to trust a brand that uses real people in their marketing. Sixty-two percent said they actively seek out brands that align with their values. This is where the market is heading, and we have a chance to lead the charge."

The CFO folded her arms, her expression unreadable. "All right, but you're still talking about shifting significant resources to this campaign. If it succeeds, fantastic. But what's the opportunity cost? Couldn't we achieve similar results with less risk?"

Punk was ready for this, too. "Opportunity cost is always a concern, but let's consider the alternative," he said, clicking to the next slide. On one side, a bar graph showed their current trajectory—modest growth but a flat trendline for market share. On the other side, there was a projection of their competitor's growth, which had skyrocketed after adopting an authenticity-first strategy.

"The cost of doing nothing is stagnation," Punk said firmly. "If we don't take steps now to differentiate ourselves, we'll lose relevance in a rapidly evolving market. This campaign isn't just about growth; it's about survival."

The Turning Point

The CFO broke the silence. "What would the initial investment look like?"

Punk quickly outlined a phased budget, emphasising efficiency and scalable growth. Questions from other executives followed—each met with Punk's well-researched answers. He didn't just defend his proposal; he used their doubts to reinforce his points.

The CEO, now visibly intrigued, asked the final question: "What's your ultimate goal here, Punk?"

"To make us more than a brand," Punk replied. "To make us a movement."

Pivoting Concerns into Momentum

Punk paused, scanning the room. He could see the gears turning in their minds. Questions were no longer defensive

– they were exploratory. He had moved the room from scepticism to cautious curiosity.

To cement his point, he concluded the section with a final slide: "The Cost of Inaction." It displayed a timeline of companies that had failed to innovate—each a former market leader that had been overtaken by bold competitors.

"Ladies and gentlemen," Punk said, his voice resolute, "this isn't just about taking a risk; it's about taking the right risk. And I firmly believe this strategy is the one that positions us for long-term success."

For a moment, the room was silent. Then the CEO nodded, a faint smile playing on his lips. "Punk," he said, "you've certainly given us something to think about."

Aftermath

When the meeting adjourned, the management team left with more than a presentation – they carried Punk's vision. Back in his office, Punk allowed himself a moment of quiet celebration. The hard work wasn't over, but the first hurdle had been cleared. He'd not only convinced the top brass but inspired them.

As he leaned back in his chair, Punk reflected: success wasn't just about great ideas. It was about belief—both in himself and the power of the story he was telling.

What did Punk do here? In summary, here are the key takeaways, or you may call, smart ways to get the green signal:

1. Be Clear and Concise

Executives don't have time for long-winded explanations. Get straight to the point. Start with a strong opening that highlights the problem, your solution, and the expected outcome. Use simple language – no jargon.

2. Show the Business Impact

Frame your proposal in terms of revenue growth, cost savings, market expansion, or efficiency improvements. Use data, case studies, or competitor insights to support your claims. Instead of saying, "This will improve customer engagement," say, "This will increase customer retention by 15%, leading to an additional £2 million in revenue."

3. Align with Company Goals

Executives care about the big picture. If your idea aligns with the company's strategic goals, they are more likely to listen. Research current business priorities and show how your proposal fits in.

4. Anticipate Objections and Have Answers Ready

Think like a sceptic. What concerns might they have? Is it cost? Execution risks? Resources? Address these issues upfront with well-thought-out solutions.

5. Use Storytelling

Facts and figures are essential, but stories make your pitch memorable. Share a brief real-life example of a competitor's success or a customer pain point your idea will solve. This makes your argument more relatable.

6. Leverage Influencers

If you can get buy-in from middle managers or respected colleagues before presenting to top management, it strengthens your case. Senior executives are more likely to listen if they know key team members support the idea.

7. Timing Matters

Avoid pitching during stressful periods like budget season or right after a major crisis. Choose a moment when executives are more open to discussion, such as during strategic planning sessions.

8. Offer a Pilot Programme

If your idea seems too risky for immediate full-scale implementation, propose a small-scale pilot. This reduces perceived risk and gives management a chance to see results before committing fully.

Persuading top management is an art that combines logic, timing, and strategy. The key is to make your case in a way that speaks to their priorities: business impact, company goals, and risk management. When you present your ideas clearly, backed by strong data and strategic alignment, your chances of getting approval increase significantly.

CHAPTER 6

In-flight Turbulence (With Oxygen Masks Sometimes)

*The turbulence (trouble) makers who keep making
Punk's life hell*

Punk knew that in the high-stakes world of marketing, troublemakers are inevitable. Whether they come from within the team, competitors, or external critics, handling them effectively can determine the success of a campaign. Here's how he managed such challenges while staying focused on executing his plan.

External Critics

As the campaign rolled out on social media, a storm of negative comments hit his team's radar. Some were constructive – questions about ingredient sourcing and pricing. Others, however, were blatant troublemaking.

"Another overpriced scam targeting people's insecurities," one commenter wrote on Instagram.

Punk leaned over his digital strategist's desk, reviewing the comments. "We don't delete critiques unless they violate guidelines," he said. "Instead, **let's address them head-on**." This was a masterstroke.

He crafted a response strategy. For every genuine concern, Punk's team provided transparent answers. When asked about the price point, they explained, "Our products are formulated with premium, dermatologist-recommended ingredients and come in refillable packaging designed to reduce waste. It's an investment in both your skin and the planet."

For outright trolling, Punk had a different approach. **"Don't feed the fire**," he advised. Instead, they used humour and positivity to deflect negativity without engaging in fruitless arguments. For instance, when one user mocked the brand's tagline, "***Glow Beyond***," the team replied with a playful, "*Thank you for noticing our shine!*"

The balance of professionalism and wit not only neutralised the troublemakers but also won over onlookers. Engagement skyrocketed, and even the sceptics started rethinking their positions.

In today's digital world, it is extremely critical to handle social media trolls smartly. It helps in:

- **Protecting Brand Reputation** – Ignoring or mishandling trolls can escalate negativity, harming the brand's image and discouraging potential customers. A well-managed response, however, showcases professionalism and composure.

- **Maintaining Customer Trust** – Genuine customers look at how brands handle criticism. A balanced approach—distinguishing between constructive feedback and trolling—demonstrates a commitment to transparency and customer care.

- **Preventing Unnecessary Controversy** – Engaging in emotional or aggressive exchanges can lead to viral negativity. A strategic, calm response can de-escalate situations while upholding the brand's integrity.

- **Encouraging Positive Engagement** – Trolls thrive on attention, but when brands focus on meaningful interactions and positive conversations, they shift the narrative towards community-building.

- **Protecting the Mental Well-Being of Teams** – Social media managers can face burnout due to constant negativity. Having clear guidelines on dealing with trolls helps maintain a healthy work environment.

Punk ticked all the above boxes!

Competitor Interference

Just as momentum began to build, Punk's campaign faced a subtle but deliberate challenge from a competitor. An established skincare brand released a press statement on the same day, touting the eco-friendly merits of its line. It was clear they were attempting to overshadow the launch.

Punk didn't panic. Instead, he viewed the situation as an opportunity. "They're validating our strategy," he told his core team. ***If the competition feels threatened enough to react, it means we're doing something right.***"

He pivoted quickly, deciding to highlight his product's refillable innovation in their advertisements that same week. Using comparisons without naming the competitor, the adverts asked, "Why recycle when you can reuse? Discover the future of sustainable skincare."

The move reinforced the product's USP while subtly outmanoeuvring the competition. Punk also ensured their Public Relations (PR) team pitched exclusive interviews to beauty editors, positioning the brand as a trailblazer.

Managing Retailer Resistance

Punk's plan also included partnerships with key luxury retailers, but not all store managers were on board. Some were resistant to allocating prime shelf space for an unproven brand. And that too, when the company was focused more on online sales.

During one particularly tense meeting, the regional manager of a high-end department store voiced scepticism. "Your brand is new. Why should we prioritise it over established players?"

Punk leaned into his experience and the power of storytelling. He walked the manager through the consumer demand trends his team had meticulously analysed. "There's a gap in the market for luxury skincare that truly delivers on sustainability. Shoppers want more than promises—they want solutions. By being the only retailer, apart from the online space, to showcase, you're not just selling products; you're leading a movement."

He followed up by offering co-branded launch events and influencer collaborations exclusive to the store, sweetening the deal. By the end of the meeting, the manager agreed to pilot the brand with prominent placements.

Internal Power Struggles

Troublemakers weren't limited to external players. Even within the organisation, conflicting agendas occasionally emerged. The most notable came when the sales and branding teams clashed over messaging.

Sales wanted to push discounts during the launch week to maximise uptake, while branding feared it would cheapen the luxury image. Typical sales & marketing tussle. Does that ring any bells? I am sure it does.

Punk, sensing the sensitivity of the situation, called a meeting to mediate. "We all want the same thing – a successful launch. Let's find a way to align."

He proposed a compromise: instead of discounts, they would offer a gift-with-purchase incentive. Customers would receive a free deluxe-sized refillable cleanser with their first purchase. Punk's idea clicked and mitigated a big problem.

The solution preserved the brand's premium image while giving the sales team the tools they needed to drive conversions.

Embracing Lessons from Setbacks

Despite Punk's proactive measures, not all troublemakers could be silenced. A micro-influencer who had partnered with the brand unexpectedly went off-script during a live review, criticising the product's scent.

Punk immediately contacted the influencer to address their concerns. "*We appreciate your honesty,*" he said. "*We'll take the feedback to our product team.*"

He also spun the incident into an opportunity. The brand issued a social media post acknowledging the feedback: "*We're listening. Scent preferences are personal, and we're exploring additional fragrance-free options for the future.*"

The response was met with applause from the audience, who appreciated the brand's transparency and willingness to evolve.

Celebrating Wins and Moving Forward

By the end of the campaign, Punk's ability to handle all the challenges and the troublemakers had proven critical to the brand's success. The new brand secured unprecedented customer acceptance, a high share of online sales, placements in major retailers, amassed a loyal online following, and exceeded all the sales projections for the first quarter.

Reflecting on the journey, Punk shared his insights with his team during a celebratory dinner. **"Troublemakers are inevitable,"** he said, raising his glass. **"But they're also opportunities in disguise. They challenge us to think smarter, act faster, and be better."**

As the team cheered, Punk smiled. He knew the real victory lay not just in launching a successful brand but in building a resilient team and a brand ethos that could weather any storm.

Managing troublemakers during a marketing campaign requires a combination of patience, strategy and adaptability. By engaging sceptics, addressing criticism constructively and staying focused on the brand's goals, Punk not only navigated challenges but strengthened his campaign. For him, every troublemaker was a chance to refine the strategy and showcase the brand's resilience.

CHAPTER 7

The Balancing Act

The art of navigating turbulence and landing with flying colours

Crisis management is not about avoiding crises altogether – that's impossible. Instead, it's about handling them efficiently with minimal damage. Your ability to respond swiftly, communicate effectively, and show accountability determines how quickly you can recover and regain trust. Preparedness is key – because in business, a crisis is never a question of 'if" but 'when'. Let us see what kind of crisis awaits Punk and how he navigates through it.

Punk had executed the campaign by navigating all sorts of external and internal challenges. As the results started coming in, the campaign was regarded as a successful one. But something happened just before the curtain went down.

Crisis in the Spotlight

The office buzzed with an unease that could almost be felt, as though the fluorescent lights themselves had dimmed. The whispers started early—little ripples of confusion cascading through the sales and marketing teams. Punk sensed it before he even got the call. It was instinct. For days, the campaign had soared; his vision had been validated, his team energised, and numbers were finally proving the strategy's worth. However, marketing, as Punk knew better than anyone, was a balancing act. A single misstep could send even the most carefully crafted campaign wobbling.

That misstep had come in the form of Jenna Rae.

Jenna Rae wasn't just another social media influencer—she was the influencer. With two million engaged followers, her face had practically become synonymous with the campaign's authenticity-first message. Her posts about using the brand's new skincare line had gone viral, her words dripping with genuine enthusiasm and effortless credibility.

Except now, Jenna Rae had turned.

Her latest video was a stark contrast to the glowing testimonials that had fuelled the campaign's early success. Sitting against a minimalist backdrop, Jenna looked directly into the camera and said with practised sincerity, *"I've always promised to be real with you guys, and after using the products from [Competition], I feel like I've finally found my perfect match. I owe it to you to share what works best for me."*

And with that, a well-loved face that once vouched for Punk's brand now openly endorsed their biggest competitor. The fallout was immediate.

The Growing Crisis

Punk sat in the conference room as his team scrambled through the repercussions. "We're haemorrhaging trust," said Camilia, his head of PR, scanning social sentiment on her tablet. "Her video has racked up over half a million views in eight hours. The comment section is chaos—our credibility is being questioned, and some customers are saying Jenna Rae misled them earlier."

"Sales in our flagship markets have slowed," added Aaron from analytics. "Web traffic is flatlining, and initial projections for this week are taking a hit. If we don't act fast, this could spiral."

Punk listened quietly. The room was filled with worried energy. Each person at the table was ready to react, to strike back or counterattack. But Punk's mind worked differently. Reacting without clarity was the fastest way to give fuel to a fire. He leaned back in his chair, exuding calm even as his thoughts raced.

"Okay," he said finally. "Here's what we're not going to do – we're not going to panic."

Analysing the Situation

Punk rose to his feet and clicked the projector on, pulling up Jenna Rae's video. He played it once more, but this time, he muted the sound. "Look at this," he said, pointing to the screen. "This isn't about us. Jenna isn't bashing our product—she's promoting another one. That's important. It's subtle, but the narrative isn't that our brand failed. It's just that she's moved on."

The team looked at him quizzically, but he continued. "We're not dealing with a scandal, just a credibility gap. She was one voice in our larger campaign, albeit an important one. We can't let her influence define the success of everything we've built. What's our story? Real people, real results. That hasn't changed. Jenna Rae is one voice out of many."

Controlling the Narrative

Punk shifted the conversation. "Step one is controlling the narrative. We can't win this fight on Jenna's turf – we need to refocus attention back on our customers and their stories. Camilia, I want an immediate amplification of user-generated content."

Camilia nodded, already taking notes.

"Pull out testimonials from customers who've seen real results with our products. Highlight the micro-influencers and community voices who are still with us. If Jenna's post is the storm, our customer stories are the calm. We flood the channels with authenticity. Instagram, TikTok, YouTube—everywhere she's being talked about, we redirect the conversation."

In my own experience as well, in the chaos of a crisis, words can feel like weapons—careless ones can unravel trust, and silence can deepen wounds. But controlling the narrative isn't about shouting the loudest; it's about speaking the clearest. It's the art of holding onto truth when the world tries to twist it into something it's not.

Imagine standing in a storm—wild winds hurl doubts, accusations, and noise. The instinct is to fight back, to scream over the noise. But the strongest voices are steady. 'Controlling the narrative is not about reacting to every gust; it's about planting your feet and letting the storm pass around you.' It's speaking with confidence when others waver, sharing your truth with calm clarity, and trusting that people will see through the chaos.

In moments of doubt, you don't fight for attention—you fight for trust. You amplify what's real: stories, results, and the quiet voices of those who still believe. A single storm doesn't define you; it tests you. **Controlling the narrative is knowing who you are and proving it, not with noise, but with proof.**

When the dust settles, those who stayed true to themselves are the ones still standing. And those who listened? They'll remember the calm in your voice.

Let us come back to Punk.

Reinforcing Trust

Punk turned to the analytics team. "Aaron, I want data—proof of performance. We've got before-and-after results from actual users, right? Compile it into a clean, easy-to-understand infographic series that proves the efficacy of our products. We'll share those visuals across our channels."

"What about paid ads?" Camilia asked.

Punk paused, thinking. "We'll go light on paid for now. If we pour money into pushing back, it'll look desperate. This needs to feel organic. We want our real customers to stand up for us. And they will—because our product works."

He pointed back at the muted video on the screen. "Jenna Rae isn't the first influencer to change sides, and she won't be the last. Consumers are smart – they'll know this isn't about loyalty to a product; it's business. What matters is our transparency and our results."

The Bold Move: Turning Loss into Opportunity

The room was calmer now, but Punk wasn't done. He walked to the whiteboard and drew a circle. "Now, let's talk about turning this into an opportunity. What if, instead of ignoring Jenna, we leaned into the conversation—on our terms?"

The team looked uncertain, but Punk's confidence was unwavering. "We release a short-form video campaign featuring micro-influencers and loyal customers, but here's the twist: one of them says something along the lines of, 'Sometimes people move on, but for me, this is what works. And I'm staying.' We address Jenna Rae's departure without ever naming her. It's subtle, confident, and keeps the spotlight on our community."

"Won't that feel like we're being passive-aggressive?" Camilia asked carefully.

"Not if we do it right," Punk replied. "Tone is everything. Make it calm, honest, and positive. We're not bitter. We're not petty. We're simply saying: 'We're here for the people who believe in us.' That's a message consumers respect."

Execution and Response

Over the next 48 hours, Punk's strategy went into overdrive. The PR team flooded social media with uplifting stories from real users – testimonials, images, and videos celebrating genuine results. Micro-influencers rallied around the brand, posting content that felt authentic and heartfelt.

The highlight was the short-form campaign Punk spearheaded, titled "What Works for You?" In one particularly compelling clip, a young woman with glowing skin looked directly at the camera and said, "Hey, skincare's personal. I get it. But for me, this works. And I'm sticking with it."

The campaign struck the perfect balance of confidence and class. Consumers noticed, and the tide began to turn. Comments under Jenna Rae's video started shifting. Followers began saying:

- "Brands evolve, and influencers move on, but I've had great results with this product."

- "I love how they handled this. No drama—just proof."

The competitor's brief victory was overshadowed by the steady resilience of Punk's campaign. By keeping the focus on results, community, and authenticity, he managed to weather the influencer's departure without derailing months of hard work.

The Reflection

Two weeks later, Punk sat in his office reviewing the updated numbers. Sales had stabilised. Engagement was strong. Customer sentiment was trending back in the right direction. Camilia walked in, grinning. "Jenna Rae's video is old news. Our customer stories are outperforming hers now."

Punk leaned back in his chair, exhaling deeply. He knew the work was far from over, but this win was particularly satisfying. Marketing, he reminded himself, wasn't about perfection – it was about adaptation. And when the unexpected happened, the brands that stayed true to their core values were the ones that survived.

"Crisis averted," Camilia said, handing him a report. Punk smiled. "No, crisis managed."

After a turbulent and dreadful experience, Punk's flight had landed safely. And we can surely say, 'with flying colours'.

CHAPTER 8

Making a Lasting Impact

Turning the Spotlight Inward

– Douglas Smith

Punk leaned back in his chair; his eyes fixed on the final campaign report glowing on his laptop screen. The numbers were better than he could have hoped for—website traffic was up by 300%, conversion rates were the highest in the company's recent history, and social media engagement was off the charts. The launch had not only created a buzz in the market but had established the skincare brand as a credible and exciting player. It was a textbook win.

Yet, Punk knew that success didn't just live in PowerPoint slides or analytics dashboards. To him, real success meant earning acknowledgement, not just from external audiences but from the people within the company. After all, internal recognition was fuel—it sparked pride, motivation, and alignment across every department. A marketing triumph wasn't just his victory; it belonged to the whole organisation. But first, they needed to *see* it.

Punk stood up, paced to the window, and began thinking about how he could tell this story—*the* story of the campaign's success—in a way that resonated across all levels of the company. He needed to do internal PR, and he needed to do it smartly.

The 'WHY' behind internal PR

The first rule of communication, Punk reminded himself, was that people need to know the *why*. Why should someone in the finance team care about a marketing campaign? Why would the IT department or HR celebrate this launch's success?

Punk scribbled in his notebook:

1. *Marketing impacts revenue and growth.*

2. *Marketing wins help build the brand everyone works for.*

3. *Celebrating success boosts morale and brings departments together.*

   "If you can connect this success to what matters to each team, you're not just talking about a campaign—you're telling a story they care about," Punk thought to himself.

He had his strategy in mind. Now, it was time to execute it like he would any external campaign: with a clear message, the right tools, and a big dose of creativity.

Crafting the Story

Punk gathered his team in the creative war room, a space filled with whiteboards, sticky notes, and half-empty coffee cups.

"Alright, folks, we've crushed this campaign, but the job isn't done yet," Punk started, his voice calm but full of purpose. "We're going to run an *internal* campaign now. Everyone in this company needs to know about the success we just pulled off. Why? Because this isn't just a marketing win—it's a win for every team, every department, and every person who helped us make it happen."

Camilia, his head of PR, raised an eyebrow. "Internal PR, huh? How do we make people care?"

Punk grinned. "We tell the story the way we'd tell any good story. We focus on impact, make it relatable, and celebrate the people who contributed. If they feel connected to it, they'll care. So here's what we're going to do."

He wrote three words on the board: *Results. Recognition. Connection.*

1. **Results:** Share the campaign's success metrics in a simple, exciting way.

2. **Recognition:** Celebrate the teams and people who made this launch possible.

3. **Connection:** Show how this success aligns with the company's larger vision and future goals.

"People need to see the numbers, feel the pride, and understand the bigger picture," Punk said, turning back to his team. "We'll make sure of it."

Choosing the Medium

Punk knew he needed to deliver this message through multiple channels—because internal communication, much like marketing, needed the right touchpoints.

1. The All-Hands Presentation

The cornerstone of the internal PR plan would be an all-hands meeting. A big, splashy event where Punk could tell the story of the campaign's success step by step.

He outlined the presentation:

- Start with an attention-grabbing visual—like a "before and after" slide showing the staggering growth in website traffic and sales.

- Share the *story* of the campaign: the strategy, the challenges faced, and how the team overcame them.

- Highlight the numbers: revenue impact, engagement, and customer response.

- Connect it to company-wide goals—how this win proves the brand is on track for even bigger achievements.

- End with gratitude: call out specific teams—R&D, product, sales, IT, customer support—and explain how their work contributed to the success.

Punk planned to keep it sharp, engaging, and filled with energy. "No corporate droning allowed," he muttered to himself as he outlined the flow.

2. A Company-Wide Email Campaign

Not everyone could make it to the all-hands meeting, and Punk knew some people preferred reading to listening. He decided on a series of celebratory emails:

- **Email 1:** *"Big News: Our Skincare Launch Was a Smash!"*—A high-energy summary of the success, with colourful visuals and key metrics front and centre.

- **Email 2:** *"Meet the Heroes Behind the Win"*—Spotlighting key players and teams, with personal quotes and photos.

- **Email 3:** *"What's Next?"*—Connecting this success to future opportunities, hinting at how the company can build on this momentum.

The emails would be brief, visually exciting and impossible to ignore.

3. The Intranet and Social Proof

Punk knew employees spent time on the company's internal platform. He'd use it to share behind-the-scenes content: videos of the campaign team brainstorming, testimonials from customers who loved the product, and "Did You Know?" posts highlighting fun facts about the campaign's success.

Additionally, Punk planned to invite employees to share their own thoughts. "What does this launch mean to you? What part of the campaign excited you the most?" Encouraging engagement would make people feel part of the celebration.

4. Office Visuals and Swag

To bring the celebration to life, Punk would work with HR to deck out common areas with campaign posters and success visuals—graphs, quotes, and smiling customer photos. He also ordered branded swag: mugs, tote bags, and notebooks that read, *"Success Starts with Us."* Small, tangible reminders that the win belonged to everyone.

Executing with Energy

The following week, Punk stood on the brightly lit stage of the all-hands meeting, with a packed audience staring up at him and more employees streaming the presentation online.

"Before we jump in, I want you all to remember one thing," Punk began, his voice filled with warmth and pride. "Every one of you played a role in what I'm about to show you."

He clicked the first slide, and the numbers appeared on the screen: growth percentages, engagement spikes, and glowing customer feedback. A gasp rippled through the crowd, followed by applause.

"This is what happens when we come together," Punk continued, walking across the stage. "R&D gave us an incredible product. The sales team put it in the right hands. IT made sure the website never crashed. And customer service—*you* kept customers smiling. This campaign was a team effort, and *this*"—he pointed at the screen— "is your success."

He ended the presentation by playing a short video – a vibrant montage of customers showing off the product, real people experiencing real results. It was fun, human, and celebratory. As the screen faded to black, the applause was thunderous.

The Impact

Over the next few days, the energy from the campaign spread like wildfire. Employees posted photos of their swag on internal channels, sharing messages of pride:

- *"Amazing to see what our marketing team pulled off! Proud to be part of this company."*

- *"Success feels sweeter when you see how hard everyone worked for it."*

The email campaign reinforced the message, and comments poured in on the intranet, with employees congratulating one another and sharing how excited they were for what came next.

Punk sat in his office, watching the messages roll in, a satisfied smile on his face. The campaign's success wasn't just external anymore. By telling the story internally, he had turned it into a rallying point – a moment of pride that united the company.

"Good work deserves to be seen," he whispered to himself. "And now, everyone knows."

CHAPTER 9

The End Game
(or Just the beginning)

*What did the whole experience mean for Punk, and
what are his ambitions*

Punk checked his watch as he stepped into the executive lounge, a sleek and quiet corner of the corporate headquarters. This wasn't his usual stomping ground—he thrived in brainstorming rooms filled with noise, post-its, and the buzz of creative energy. But today was different. The CEO had invited him for coffee, an invitation that was both an honour and a bit unnerving. CEOs rarely invited mid-level marketers for casual chats unless something significant was on their minds.

"Relax, Punk," he muttered to himself as he adjusted his shirt collar. The campaign had been a roaring success; the numbers couldn't lie, and his internal PR had spread that success like wildfire across the company. But still, when the head of the company wanted a one-on-one, it was hard to ignore the little flutter of nerves.

"Punk!" came a warm voice that broke his thoughts.

Punk turned to see David Westwood, the CEO, approaching with a broad smile. David was a tall, distinguished man in his mid-fifties, his silver hair a sharp contrast to the relaxed, modern cut of his blazer. He didn't carry the air of a distant executive; instead, his energy was approachable, with a knack for putting people at ease. That said, the weight of his presence wasn't lost on anyone.

"Mr. Westwood," Punk greeted with a nod.

"David, please," the CEO corrected him quickly with a smile. "We're here for coffee, not a boardroom presentation."

Punk chuckled nervously and followed David to a sunlit corner table where two freshly brewed cups of coffee awaited them. The rich aroma filled the space, and Punk felt himself relax just a little as he sat down.

The CEO's Take on the Campaign's Success

David lifted his cup, took a small sip, and looked directly at Punk. "First things first, I want to congratulate you, Punk. You and your team pulled off something extraordinary with this launch. It was one of the most well-executed campaigns I've seen in my time here."

Punk's shoulders eased, and a smile crept onto his face. "Thank you, David. That means a lot coming from you."

David set his cup down and leaned slightly forward, the gesture signalling that this wasn't just idle praise. "Let me tell you what I loved most about this campaign. Yes, the numbers are impressive—phenomenal, actually. But beyond the analytics, what stood out to me was the way you handled the brand narrative.

The strategy wasn't just about getting customers to buy skincare products; it was about creating trust, delivering value, and starting conversations."

Punk nodded, feeling a swell of pride. He had poured his heart into crafting not just a marketing plan but a story that resonated.

"That influencer hiccup—Jenna Rae, right?" David continued. "I watched how you managed to steer the ship without getting defensive. You doubled down on authenticity, amplified real voices, and turned a potential crisis into an opportunity to reinforce our brand values. That was masterful work."

"Thank you, David," Punk replied sincerely. "We knew we couldn't control every narrative, but we could stay true to what the brand stands for. People see through the noise if you give them something real to believe in."

David smiled again. "Exactly. Brands that endure don't chase trends—they build trust. You understood that instinctively. The work you've done is more than a successful launch. It's an example of how marketing, when done well, becomes a cornerstone of the business."

Punk's chest swelled at the words. For someone like David to recognise the bigger picture meant more to him than he had expected.

What Success Meant for Punk

David leaned back in his chair, studying Punk with curiosity. "So, tell me, Punk, what does success look like to you? I mean, beyond the metrics and awards. What drives you?"

Punk paused, caught slightly off guard by the question. He wrapped his hands around the warm cup of coffee and stared into it for a moment, gathering his thoughts.

"I think success, for me, has always been about impact," he started slowly, then looked up. "I didn't get into marketing just to sell products. I got into it because I believe in the power of storytelling—stories that inspire people, solve problems and make life better in some small way."

David nodded thoughtfully, encouraging him to go on.

"When I look at this campaign, sure, the numbers are great, and I'm proud of that. But what really matters to me is the way we connect with people. Seeing customers post about how our product made them feel confident and seeing the community engage with our message—that's success. It's creating something meaningful that doesn't feel forced or transactional."

He paused again and smiled. "Success also means proving to myself that I can deliver. Every time I take on a new project, there's this quiet voice in the back of my head asking, 'Can you really pull this off?' When I do, it's not about ego. It's about pushing myself to do better, to think smarter, and to create work that's worth remembering."

David's eyes glimmered with understanding. "Impact over vanity metrics. I like that. You've got the heart of a storyteller, Punk, and that's rare. Many marketers chase clicks and views—few chase meaning."

Punk let the words settle over him. Validation, from the very top, felt incredibly grounding.

Punk's Future Ambitions

David tapped his fingers lightly against the table, as if weighing his next words. "So, where do you go from here, Punk? What's next for you?"

Punk grinned at the question. He'd been waiting for this.

"Honestly, David, I want to keep building. I've spent years learning the ropes—understanding markets, people, and brands. But I want to start thinking bigger."

"Bigger?" David prompted, intrigued.

"Yes," Punk replied, leaning forward now. "I want to help shape not just campaigns but the future of this brand. We've proven what we can do when we lead with trust and authenticity. Now, I want to take that further—think about how this brand can grow into new spaces, new markets, and even new products. I want to challenge myself to think like a business leader, not just a marketer."

David raised an eyebrow. "That sounds ambitious and exciting."

"It is," Punk said with confidence. "I love the creative side of marketing, but I also want to understand how we tie that creativity to long-term business strategy. I want to sit at the table where decisions about the future are made and bring a perspective that combines storytelling, strategy, and customer insight."

David nodded slowly, a thoughtful smile forming. "You know, Punk, many people in your position are content with winning campaigns and annual bonuses. It's refreshing to hear someone who's thinking bigger. Ambition is good—when it's grounded."

Punk smiled back. "I don't want to just play in my lane. I want to help this company win – in every way."

David studied him for a moment, as though considering something. "Well, Punk, you've proven you can deliver results. And I like people who can deliver and think big. Keep this fire going. You've got the makings of someone who could help steer this company's future."

Punk blinked, a flicker of surprise passing over his face. That sounded a lot like an open door – an opportunity.

"Thank you, David," he said, keeping his composure. "I'm ready to prove myself."

"Let me give you a piece of advice, Punk," David said, his tone steady and deliberate. "Ambition is a powerful thing—but only if it's guided by clarity and patience. You're already proving that you can deliver results and inspire teams. That's step one. The next step is building influence."

Punk listened intently.

"Influence isn't about titles or hierarchy; it's about trust and consistency. If you want to help shape the company's future, start by showing up as someone who understands not just marketing but the business as a whole. Learn what drives revenue, what challenges the other departments face, and how decisions ripple across the organisation. When you can connect the dots between creativity and business outcomes, people will listen."

David's gaze locked onto Punk's. "Take the time to learn. Be curious. Seek out mentors beyond marketing. You'll be pleasantly surprised to see yourself transform into a business leader and not just a marketer."

Punk had the best day in office so far. He knew this conversation over coffee was going to change his life, and he was on the path to becoming a great and influential leader.

CHAPTER 10

Success Mantra

What made Punk so successful?

Roger Federer

Punk wasn't your average marketer. From the moment he stepped into the world of brand strategies and advertising, it was clear he had something special. He didn't just check boxes; he broke them, rearranged them, and sometimes turned them into art pieces. But what exactly made Punk a successful marketer? Was it his knack for understanding trends? His ability to charm a room full of sceptical executives? Or was it something deeper? Let's dive into the elements that made Punk a standout in his field.

1. A Love for Storytelling

If you asked Punk what marketing meant to him, he'd smile and say, "It's just storytelling but with a purpose." And he meant it. Punk had an innate ability to craft narratives that resonated with people. Whether it was a skincare campaign or a product launch, he didn't focus solely on the features or benefits. Instead, he created stories that touched emotions and built connections.

Take the skincare launch campaign as an example. Instead of bombarding audiences with statistics about ingredients and efficacy, Punk told the story of a young professional regaining confidence after battling acne. The ad wasn't about the product; it was about the transformation. Customers saw themselves in the narrative, and that's what made it powerful.

2. The Relatable Genius

Punk had the rare gift of making complex marketing strategies sound like casual conversations. During meetings, while others threw around jargon like "KPIs" and "ecosystem synergies," Punk's explanations were refreshingly straightforward.

"We're not selling face cream," he once told his team. "We're selling the feeling of looking in the mirror and loving what you see."

This ability to simplify and humanise his ideas earned him the trust of colleagues and clients alike. He wasn't just a marketer; he was someone who could see the human side of every transaction.

3. A Data Whisperer

While Punk had a heart for storytelling, he also had a brain for analytics. Unlike many creatives who shy away from spreadsheets, Punk embraced them. To him, numbers weren't cold or intimidating; they were clues.

"Data is just people in disguise," he'd often say. "You just need to know how to listen."

He spent hours digging into reports, uncovering patterns others missed. When his team noticed a drop in online engagement, Punk traced it back to a mismatch between content tone and audience preferences. He didn't guess; he knew because the data told him.

This balance of creativity and logic sets him apart. He wasn't a marketer who relied on gut instinct alone – he was a marketer who backed his instincts with evidence.

4. The Master of Persuasion

Punk could convince a room full of sceptics that the sky was green if he needed to. His secret? He listened first and spoke second. Instead of bulldozing through objections, he acknowledged them.

When pitching his ambitious skincare campaign to the company's top brass, he faced resistance. "Why not stick to what's worked before?" one executive asked.

Punk didn't bristle. Instead, he nodded and said, "I see your point. The old approach has worked well in the past. But let me show you why this new direction isn't a gamble; it's an evolution."

By addressing concerns head-on and framing his ideas as logical progressions rather than radical leaps, Punk won over even the most cautious decision-makers.

5. Resilience in the Face of Challenges

Success in marketing isn't just about having great ideas; it's about surviving the storms. And Punk weathered plenty of them. From last-minute campaign changes to public relations hiccups, he faced his share of crises.

One notable example was when a social influencer broke his contract and started promoting a competitor's product. The news spread quickly, casting a shadow over an otherwise successful campaign. Instead of panicking, Punk saw it as an opportunity.

"Let's double down on authenticity," he told his team. "We don't need influencers to speak for us; we have real customers with real stories."

He shifted the campaign's focus, amplifying user-generated content and testimonials. Not only did the campaign recover, but it also strengthened the brand's reputation as honest and customer-centric.

6. Lifelong Curiosity

Punk never stopped learning. He'd devour books, attend webinars, and experiment with new tools just for the thrill of discovering something new. His desk was a chaotic mix of industry reports, sticky notes, and half-finished creative sketches.

"Marketing changes every day," he'd say. "If you're not learning, you're falling behind."

This curiosity wasn't limited to marketing. Punk found inspiration in art, music, and even nature. Once, he built an entire campaign around the patterns of light and shadow he noticed during a sunset. His ability to draw connections between unrelated fields gave his work a freshness that others struggled to replicate.

7. Building Relationships, Not Transactions

For Punk, marketing wasn't about pushing products; it was about building relationships. He treated customers like friends rather than sales targets. This philosophy extended to his team and colleagues as well.

"Happy teams create happy campaigns," he often said.

He took the time to know his team members personally, celebrating their wins and supporting them through challenges. When the pressure of a tight deadline loomed, Punk's positivity kept the morale high. His leadership wasn't just about delegation; it was about inspiration.

8. Staying True to His Values

In an industry where it's easy to chase trends, Punk stood firm in his values. He believed in honesty, inclusivity, and delivering genuine value to customers. These weren't just buzzwords to him; they were the foundation of every campaign he created.

"If it doesn't feel right, it probably isn't," he'd remind his team.

When a potential partnership with a controversial influencer was proposed, Punk vetoed it without hesitation. "Our brand stands for trust. This partnership would undermine that," he explained. His integrity earned him respect, even when his decisions weren't the easiest ones.

9. The Power of Internal PR

Punk understood that marketing wasn't just outward-facing. After a successful campaign, he made it a point to share the results with the entire company. But he didn't just present dry numbers; he told the story of the campaign—the challenges, the creative breakthroughs, and the customer feedback that made it all worthwhile.

This approach didn't just earn him applause; it built a culture of appreciation for marketing's role in the company's success. Punk knew that when everyone felt part of the journey, it strengthened the brand from the inside out.

10. Ambition with a Purpose

Finally, what truly set Punk apart was his vision for the future. He didn't see himself as just a marketer; he saw himself as a builder of brands, a creator of experiences, and a leader who could inspire change.

When asked about his ambitions, Punk says, "I want to create work that lasts. Campaigns come and go, but the way you make people feel? That's timeless."

This sense of purpose fuelled everything he did. It wasn't about personal glory; it was about leaving a legacy.

Punk's journey as a marketer wasn't defined by any single trait but by the unique combination of all these elements.

He was a storyteller, a strategist, a leader, and, most importantly, a human who understood other humans. That's what made him successful. And if you asked him, he'd just smile and say, "I'm just getting started."

The Conclusion

We evolve as individuals every single day of our life. Each one of us. Whether it is the personal side or the professional one. The same happened to me as a professional marketer. What you went through while reading the above ten chapters in this book is the summation of my experiences working with many different individuals in their personal as well as professional capacities. They are my learnings, told from Punk's perspective.

The flight that Punk took from take-off to triumph is not just one journey; it is the ultimate outcome of his various encounters, some of which turned out to be successful and many as failures. In actual life, we fail more than we succeed. The important thing is to take each failure as a stepping stone towards the success that we want. The book weaved these multiple experiences of failures and successes into one story to drive the message across to you and bring you home.

While you embark on your professional journey, or if you are already on it, I am sure you will find these experiences relatable, and there is something that will help you prepare for the unforeseen. Just keep your learning hat on. Always!

In his recent speech, the champion Roger Federer said some really profound words. This speech was packed with wisdom that goes far beyond the tennis court, offering valuable lessons for anyone navigating life's challenges and triumphs.

What stayed with me are the following lines:

"In tennis, as in life, you will lose points, matches, and even entire seasons. The key is to not let these speed bumps bring you down. Accept and learn from your losses, and look forward. It's natural, when you're down, to doubt yourself and to feel sorry for yourself. But negative energy is wasted energy. You want to become a master at overcoming hard moments. That is, to me, the sign of a champion. ***The best in the world are not the best because they win every point. It's because they know they lose again and again and have learned how to deal with it.*** *You accept it, cry it out if you need to, and then force a smile. You move on. Be relentless. Adapt and grow. Work harder. Work smarter."*

That is it from my side for this book. I wish each one of you valuable learning and great success. Keep learning and keep growing. Good luck!